61

ONE OF THE MAIN STREETS OF PORT-AU-PRINCE

HAITI

ITS DAWN OF PROGRESS AFTER
YEARS IN A NIGHT OF REVOLUTION

J. DRYDEN KUSER

NEGRO UNIVERSITIES PRESS
WESTPORT, CONNECTICUT

Originally published in 1921
by R. G. Badger, Boston

Reprinted 1970 by
Negro Universities Press
A Division of Greenwood Press, Inc.
Westport, Conn.

SBN 8371-3294-0

PRINTED IN UNITED STATES OF AMERICA

TO MY WIFE

BROOKE RUSSELL KUSER

THE SOURCE OF MY ORIGINAL INTEREST IN HAITI
AND A NEVER-TIRING AID IN THE PRESENT WORK.

INTRODUCTION

HAITI is a country of rapidly changing conditions. Like others, emerging from revolution and disorder to peace and the pursuits of peace, it finds its possibilities unlimited. Furthermore, under the Haitian-American treaty, part of the government is being run by the Haitians themselves in the three departments: executive, legislative and judicial; and a portion is controlled by the United States, including the military. In such a two-party control, there is naturally friction and this causes frequent and changing disagreements.

Whereas in January, 1920, the bandit trouble was serious, I have just found, during a brief November trip, that this has ceased to be an active danger. In its place there has arisen, not a military worry, but a political one.

Haitian agitators, supported by ill-advised Americans, have spread propaganda favoring the withdrawal of the United States from Haiti. Included in this propaganda have been the absurd accusations against the marines of cruelty toward the natives.

The question of any cruelty or unnecessary killings has been conclusively disproven by the findings of a Court of Inquiry sent to Haiti, and which has recently published its findings. As to the withdrawal of the United States from Haiti—such a course would be a menace to the world and a sad neglect of duty by the United States. Any American acquainted with Haitian conditions will agree that the marines would scarcely have boarded the American ships before the entire country would be in a state of civil war, the lives and property of foreigners endangered, and the possibility of Haiti paying off her foreign debt would be lost.

Introduction

As opposed to this prospect of revolution, we have a bright future for Haiti, if the United States remains. The country is naturally rich in its products and its soil, and labor is able to work for cheaper wages than elsewhere. This is a great incentive for American business to invest its capital, which means that the country will rapidly become rich again—as it once was in the French days. But unlike conditions in those days, the Haitian himself will share in the future development and wealth.

J. Dryden Kuser.

Bernardsville, New Jersey.

CONTENTS

LIST OF ILLUSTRATIONS

List of Illustrations

HAITI

HAITI

I

SARGASSO AND FLYING FISH

FOR the first two days out of New York harbor flocks of Herring Gulls followed us and occasionally an odd Robin and a pair of Goldfinches appeared. But after Hatteras was passed and the sea was calmer the gulls left us and flying fish took their place. Stationed at the bow I watched them dart out of the foam and skim, sometimes a few feet, often many yards. At night I took the same post and the phosphorescent "stars of the sea" shone very green against the yellow constellations above.

By the third day ever-increasing quantities of sargasso weed appeared and floated past. Torn from their beds along tropical coasts, these bits of weed act as the shelter for multifarious forms of aquatic life which live as long as the weed lives and die when it finally decays. And so, although no sign of bird or other life appeared above the water surface, we were surrounded every moment by thousands of individuals of dozens of species.

Our ship was the "Advance" of the American government-controlled Panama R. R. Steamship Company, which operates the service between New York, Haiti and Panama. Two steamers run to Panama via Port-au-Prince, Haiti, three are exclusively for Haitian ports, while the others do not stop at Haiti en route to Panama. Beside the Panama line

SIFTING COFFEE ALONG A PRINCIPAL STREET

there is the Dutch line of boats which runs
from New York to Haiti on regular sailings,
but aside from these two there are no other
lines which regularly run ships to Haiti. And
so the quickest way of travelling from Haiti
to another of the West Indies is via Panama.

Coming south, the first land appeared on
the fourth day, when the lighthouse of San
Salvador, re-named Watling's Island by the
British, showed the northern point of land
long before the rest of the flat surface was
visible. Bird Rock, the Fortune Islands and
Castle Island were passed during the next
twelve hours, and finally the high mountains
of eastern Cuba were twenty miles off our
starboard. Before these were out of sight,
the peak of Mole St. Nicholas, Haiti, arose
on the port bow. But we were by no means
yet at Port-au-Prince, our destination, for it
is a seven-hour sail from this point to the harbor in the lower part of the bay. The bay

itself is over 100 miles long, and in the center of it is the Island of Gonave, 10 by 40 miles, to which all convicts were exiled from Haiti in the French days, and many of whose present inhabitants are descendents of these exiles.

After we had passed Gonave, the mountain ranges on both sides became very close and we could see the smoke of many fires high up on their slopes. These fires, we later found out, were those of the charcoal burners, who play an important rôle on the island. The charcoal is obtained by placing the wood which has been gathered under a covering of earth in such a way as to eliminate the undesired gases and leave the charcoal. After sufficient time, the earth is removed and the charcoal carried for miles into town on the backs of "burros." Charcoal is used entirely in Haiti for kitchen fuel. Of the fires we saw in the hills, all were probably not those of charcoal burners, as it is the common thing for the natives to burn off a section of the land which they desire to use and to ascribe the fire to spontaneous combustion.

At last the vari-colored lights of Port-au-Prince peeped forth from among the foothills on the right and we followed the channel in by alignment with two huge red range lights, one on the top of the Cathedral and the other on Fort National. The beauty of coming into Port-au-Prince is by daylight, when, not unlike Serrento, it shows a background of 2800 foot mountains rising behind, and with the pellucid green sea stretching out from the town. A Haitian launch came alongside for the custom officials to board. Our passports were taken to be kept for overnight and recorded, and we were then allowed to proceed to the dock which is at the end of a long pier jutting out from the land.

As we spun along to the house where we were to visit we went over streets smoother and wider than all but a few in the United States. These streets, throughout most of the town, were put down under contract with an American firm in 1914, before American occupation of Haiti, and are of excellent quality. From the business district we came out into the Champ de Mars, a laid-out park with a bronze of Dessalines, the "Founder of Haitian Independence," in the center; and at the end a grandstand from which to watch the sports or national festivities. Next to the Champ de Mars is the new palace of the President of Haiti. It is now at a stage of near-completion, and one wing is already occupied by the President and his family. This building is the fourth palace to be built on the same site, one of the others having been set on fire and destroyed, and the other two ruined through explosions. In the latter cases the President had been unable to trust anyone with the keeping of the national supply of ammunition and was forced to keep it in his own palace, so that in both cases the Presidents were killed by means of their own powder. On the lower side of the palace are the marine barracks and the gendarme caserne, opposite one another, and above the Champ de Mars is the marine brigade headquarters.

At this point starts the residential section of the town for both wealthy Haitians and Americans and other foreigners. We rode over narrow, quaint streets, after passing the marine headquarters, until we came to Avenue Christophe and our house, of old French style and with peaked roof, which was at one time used as the Presidential palace. Most of the houses of Port-au-Prince are of this old French style and show few traces of the original Spanish. Around all the better houses there are dense tropical growths with mangoes, oranges, and guanavena or sour-sap hanging over the porches. Many of the yards have also one or two royal palms, with their great white trunks reaching over fifty feet and with leaves clustered at the top. At the very tip of the tree's trunk is the heart, for which many trees are cut down, as "heart of palm" is one of the delicacies of the tropics. In the country districts both the royal and cocoanut palm are common. The two are somewhat similar but can be easily told apart by the crooked growth of the latter and also its darker and rougher trunk.

The first morning after our arrival was cloudy, which was very unusual, for thruout the year in Port-au-Prince the mornings are almost invariably clear. So is the remainder of the day for the six months during the dry season, but in the wet season it regularly rains a downpour for about two hours late each afternoon. November is the beginning of the dry season, so for a couple of weeks after our arrival it would still occasionally rain for a few moments a day. But we missed having any of the truly tropical rains which during the summer flood the streets and sweep all before them.

While the winter is for Port-au-Prince and southern Haiti the dry season, the conditions are exactly reversed in the northern half of the republic. There the wet season commences in November, to last for six months until the next summer when all becomes dry again. And so there is never a time in Haiti when half of the island is not being well-watered and the fruit and crops in season.

II

CACOS

ALTHOUGH, in the days of the French, Cap Haitien was the capital of Haiti, to-day Port-au-Prince is the capital as well as the most important town. It is also the most modern town, being the only one, for example, to have the paved streets which I have referred to. In addition it has a good telephone and electric lighting system.

The first morning's tour of the shops in Port-au-Prince made my former knowledge of fair prices useless. Goods which it was necessary to import from the United States, such as silks and American-made cloths, seemed exorbitant; perfumes and French clothes, imported directly from Paris at a low

DESSALINES
In the Champs de Mars

THE "OPEN" MARKET JUST BELOW THE CATHEDRAL

rate of duty sold at a considerably reduced
rate from the New York price; but naturally
the greatest difference in cost was those of
native goods. Mahogany grows plentifully
throughout the interior of Haiti and hence is
easily obtained. Its price is consequently low
and I purchased a solid mahogany small dinner table for $6, which is the customary price.
But compare the price for such a piece in New
York! And then of course the native fruits
were either free along the roads or at a nominal
price in the markets. Alligator pears, bought
as a luxury in New York for 75 cents or a dollar apiece, sell in Port-au-Prince for 5 pears
for 2 cents.

In Port-au-Prince there are two markets,
the "open" and the "closed," of which the
latter is a roofed and walled structure and the
former held without cover on an open plaza,
directly beneath the wall around the Cathedral. Here, together with alligator pears, are

sold bananas, limes, grapefruit, fish, meats, dry goods and odds and ends which are found in a department store. Here also *"rapadou"* —a native candy made from brown sugar and cocoanut—is for sale. This candy is also peddled along the streets and trays full of it are carried by the natives on their heads, whilst they continually call attention to their ware by calling it out at frequent intervals. Whatever a Haitian has to carry, be it an armchair, a piece of paper or a trayful of fine glassware, he carries it upon his head. They have in this way developed the ability to stand great weight and certainly one beneficial result is the invariably erect carriage of a Haitian caused through the necessity of always maintaining balance when he carries his goods.

Up to within a few weeks of our arrival the native shops used to remain open in the evening. When we arrived, however, they closed each night at dark. This was because of a

scare which they had recently received when
a small band of revolutionary bandits, known
throughout Haiti as "cacos," attempted to
make a raid upon the town. In the old days
of unstable government the natives had become
accustomed to the existing government falling
every time the cacos arrived, and they were
not easily led to realize last September that it
is no longer possible now that the marines are
guarding the town. And hence for weeks
after the attack the shopkeepers regularly
shut themselves up in their houses at dark
each night.

For sometime after the Americans occupied
Haiti in 1915 there were no organized uprisings, but within a year various causes have led
the wild tribes of the interior to join together
into various bands and attempt organized
raids.

The fighting of these cacos is extremely
difficult for three principal reasons; first, the

secret sympathy of some reputable and prominent Haitians and the consequent impossibility of obtaining any information from them;
second, the nature of the country which per-
mits the cacos to retreat into the mountainous
regions which are wild and contain many caves
and trails unknown to the whites; and third,
the manner in which the bandits fight. Like
the Indians they conduct a warfare of night
raids and of sniping, so that only a sort of
guerrilla war can be conducted against them.
And then too, as the cacos are not in uniform,
it is impossible to know who is or who is not
a caco, except when they are actually banded
together or carrying their arms.

But results are being slowly accomplished.
The towns are protected and guarded so that
when an attack is made it can be repulsed and
patrols sent out to round up as many of the
invaders as possible. In the interior districts
where the bandits congregate and make their

rendezvous, expeditions are being continually sent out and the country honeycombed between the different hill posts. Near L'Archahai there is a cave which, dating from the earliest records of Haitian history, has been credited as being a bandit retreat. Here the cacos are still supposed to meet and go into hiding, but as the cave is a huge opening on the side of a mountain, and inaccessible unless a rope ladder be let down from someone already there, it is quite inaccessible and impossible to attack.

In Haiti there are two different armies, so to speak. The gendarmerie or national army of Haiti consists of the enlisted men who are Haitians and of officers in charge of them who are American marines loaned to the Haitian Government, in accordance with the provisions of the treaty, to organize and train the Haitian army so as to make it an efficient fighting police force which is able to support, and preserve against attack, the existing government.

The gendarmerie have abundantly proven, in many recent cases when they have been led by American officers, that they are thoroughly trustworthy and loyal fighters. Nor is there any doubt of their courage, for they are as brave as any body of troops in the world. The gendarmerie are used for guarding a town after it has been once freed from active cacoism, and everywhere in Haiti one sees their white and red stone headquarters. The gendarmerie are also used, together with the marines, to go out into the hills on patrols for routing the cacos and clearing up the country.

The second army is the occupation force of American marines stationed in Haiti since the intervention of 1915 to preserve order and protect the nationals and property of Americans and other foreigners in the country. For those marines who are in search of real adventure and fighting, even those who were in the world war might well look with envy upon the men who are doing patrol duty among the Haitian hills. Alone or in company with the gendarmes, they have had encounters so filled with adventure that I will tell of one which occurred shortly before our arrival.

Charlemagne Massena Peralte, a man who came from the Hinche district, and of natural ability as a leader, was of anti-white sympathies and early after the American occupation associated himself with a family named Zamor in the northeast country around Hinche. One of the Zamor brothers, Oreste Zamor, was formerly a president of the republic and another was the great leader of the north and is now in the Port-au-Prince prison as a conspirator. Charlemagne rose in the caco ranks to the position of chief and was so successful in his first encounters and attempts as to make the name of Charlemagne known everywhere as the supreme caco. Charlemagne was the clever and guiding hand of all the revolutionary attacks which occurred about this time, so it became of the greatest importance to capture him. Many attempts to do this were made by the marines and the gendarmes, but on each occasion his preparation for scouts and ways of escape made it possible for him to evade them.

In October, the location of Charlemagne having been reported, two marines, officers in the gendarmerie, volunteered to capture Charlemagne. They made very careful preparations to set out with twenty gendares and disguised themselves by blackened skin and native clothes. Both of the officers spoke creole well, but naturally with some foreign accent and so it was necessary for them to speak as little as was possible. When near the place where Charlemagne was reported to be spending the day, they met the first caco outposts who stopped and questioned them. Claiming they

ENTRANCE TO THE "CLOSED" MARKET

had an important message to deliver to Charlemagne, giving the password and claiming such extreme fatigue for the two officers that these officers could barely answer the questions put to them, the party succeeded in being passed.

A second and a third guard of Charlemagne's were in the same way fooled and at last the gendarmes came to a clearing. In the center of the clearing were gathered together a group of bandits around a fire, and at the side of the fire sat a woman. Behind her there was a sort of rude throne and here sat the great Charlemagne. Scarcely had the gendarmes seen the crowd collected here when they were recognized and a signal given. The woman lept to the fire and succeeded in brushing and stamping it out. In the darkness which followed, she and her followers escaped. But hardly had the signal of detection been given when Charlemagne was the aim for the gendarme rifles, and when a new fire was lighted he was found to be dead together with a few of the crowd with him.

The belief in Haiti was a common one that Charlemagne was a supernatural being who was immune from rifle bullets or the weapons of his adversaries. In fact, he himself boasted that this was true. And so, upon his death, pictures of him were taken and these the marines spread broadcast throughout the republic to prove to all Haitians that the invulnerable Charlemagne was at last killed.

It is this kind of fighting which the marines and gendarmes have to continually do in combatting the caco trouble. After the death of Charlemagne, Benôit Batraville, who was formerly a sullen police chief in the mountain town of Mirebalais, became the caco leader. He had joined the caco ranks only shortly before Charlemagne's death, and although not nearly so clever a brigand as the supreme caco was perhaps the most intelligent and the best leader when Charlemagne died. Up to the time of my departure in February, all attempts to capture Benôit had failed but I have since heard of his killing. It was during a skirmish with the marines in which the latter penetrated to the leader's rendezvous and although every other person in the camp escaped, the officer leading the marines had the good fortune to kill Benôit.

And so another man of fair intelligence has been eliminated from the bandit forces. This has practically destroyed the caco power as an offensive force, for it is the few men whom the cacos have among them of brains which make them at all a dangerous factor. The bandits are with a few exceptions utterly ignorant and unable to lead an attack unless inspired and led by someone who has lived in the towns and developed some intelligence. To illustrate the almost unbelievable state of mentality possessed by the cacos, I will tell of the prisoners taken in one raid. After the raid the prisoners were taken back to the town to be temporarily held there awaiting trial. When the men reached the house, they were unable to walk up the stairs, as stairs were new to them. They had never seen a house of two stories before and did not know what to make of the second floor.

I have mentioned a caco attempt to raid Port-au-Prince just before our arrival, in which some of the bandits reached town. By January, over a month after we arrived, the town had again assumed its normal state, and fear of another attack was practically eliminated from the minds of the natives. This was the condition when, on the morning of January 15th, the telephone rang at 4 a.m. and we heard that "3,000 cacos are marching into town by the Hasco Road." The cacos, advancing into town in column and with flags and conch-horns blowing, divided, a quarter of a mile from town, one column going along the water front and reaching town by way of the slaughter house, the other two columns turning farther inland and advancing around Belleair hill, by the radio station.

When the troops had nearly reached town our marines opened fire with Brownings and machine guns, but the natives broke ranks and fired from around corners, and rushing into the houses, fired upon the marines from the windows. Gradually they were driven back, but *en route* they had fired some of the native *"cailles,"* in the poor section of the town and the light from this lit up the entire surrounding country.

By daybreak many cacos were lying dead along the entrance to the city, the attack had been completely repulsed and the cacos driven far from town. Over 150 were captured or killed and but three of the marines wounded, only one fatally. A large number of caco had been pressed so hard on their flanks and front that they were forced to retreat into a closed valley back of Belleair and were there almost completely wiped out by a volley of machine guns.

All during the day patrols searched the plains and outlying country. In this way they captured singly or in groups many of the brigands who were retreating to the hills. One automobile full of townsmen, arriving from Gonaïves, told of meeting the caco band, or at least part of it and only escaping by a miracle. The dents and holes made by the bullets while the car ran the gauntlet between the crowd, could be seen covering the body of the car when it came into town.

In the afternoon a house-to-house search was made in the district where the fighting occurred and, asleep in his own house, the police found and recognized Solomen Janvier.

Janvier is a man who formerly lived in Port-au-Prince in the house where he was found. But he had always been a revolutionist and for many months previous to the raid had been out in the hills with the cacos.

Janvier boasted, after he had been taken to prison, that every attack which had been made upon Port-Au-Prince during recent years had been led by him; and that in the present raid there had been three leaders leading the different sections of the caco force, but that the other two were cowards and had fled before they reached town, he alone leading the actual attack.

The number of cacos who reached the town is uncertain. First reports gave the number as 3,000, which was later reduced to 1,500, as claimed by the men at Hasco, the sugar plant of the American-Haitian Sugar Company, by which the cacos passed on their way into town. But, although there were many camp followers who never entered and engaged in the fighting, it is probable that the number of actual fighters was about 300. On the morning after the raid, our cook told me that she had heard in the market places that morning that there were 2,000,000 cacos who had entered the town and that 1,000,000 had been killed. This, I think, was the wildest rumor I heard.

On the second day someone spread the rumor that 2,000 more cacos were coming into Port-au-Prince, and as it took some time to prove the report false, there was great excitement throughout the town. I went down beyond the Champ de Mars, and, rushing in every direction, were the natives, each returning to his respective home. As soon as they reached there, the windows and doors were boarded and within a very short time every house was closed and not a person was to be seen upon the streets. And so another day was lost to business, for all of the shops had

MARINE PATROL

HILLS NEAR MIREBALAIS

been closed since the raid because of the great fear that the cacos were going to make a second attack.

In October, when the raid was made before our arrival, the cacos escaped with a loss of only a few men, but in January so many of their number were killed or captured in town and out in the plains during their retreat that it will certainly make them wary of again invading the town for a long time to come.

Benôit, himself, was in part of the fighting during the January raid, but unfortunately was among the bandits who escaped and was soon back with his followers in the Mirebalais hills, where he was eventually captured as I have related.

III

EVERY MAN'S LAND—A BIT OF HISTORY

THE Republic of Haiti consists of the western part of the island of Santo Domingo, while the eastern end constitutes the country of Santo Domingo. The latter, while it has three times the territory, claims but one-third the population of Haiti, which is to-day estimated at 2,500,000. Columbus' estimate of the combined population of what is now Haiti and Santo Domingo was as high as 2,000,000, but during the four intervening centuries the change in race has been complete. Scarcely a strain of aboriginal blood is left; and no ancestor of the present natives then even knew of the "new world." Ownership of Haiti has changed hands four times in this period, and revolution, crime and barbarism have left indelible marks on the pages of her history.

The men left in Haiti by Columbus and those who followed the pioneers from Spain have scant justification for their brutal treatment of the Indians whom they met, and among the disgraces committed by white men in their dealings with the aborigines in America, the acts of the Spaniards in Haiti and Santo Domingo were among the most deplorable.

Before long, the Spaniards, having wiped out the native Indians, were obliged to search for labor to till their soil and to search for gold. All of the metals possessed by the local redskins had been stolen by the first-comers. Turning naturally to African slaves to solve the problem of labor, the Spaniards imported the blacks in ever-increasing numbers.

The Spaniards had not long been settled in this way before they were themselves forced to contest rule over the island, for French adventurers had come into the country and by 1697 the latter were so successful that most of that portion of land now known as Haiti was recognized by the Spanish to be under French control.

The French continued the practice, commenced by the Spaniards, of introducing negro slaves and thousands were each year added to the number already settled. Rapidly Haiti became France's richest colony and the stories of the magnificent estates and the luxury in which wealthy planters and French noblemen lived are pitiful in contrast with what was so soon to follow. Pauline Bonaparte's estate near "Mon Repos" on the outskirts of Port-au-Prince lies in ruins and there remains little trace of luxury about the huge pool where once she held court and receptions at which much of the nobility of France was present. It is said that the wealthy Parisians used to send their clothes to be washed in the waters of the streams of Port-au-Prince regularly every six months because of the extraordinary bluing quality which was credited to the water.

While Haiti was thus becoming a treasure island for the French, this wealth was at the expense of the black slaves, whom the French forced into overwork by extreme punishments. And thus, while the nobility in France were holding down their peasants to vaunt their vanity in the effete displays of the court of Louis XV, and thus foster the seeds of discontent which bore such frightful fruit in the days of the Guillotine, the French planters were doing the self-same thing to a worse extent in their treatment of the blacks in Haiti. Out of their cruel servitude was to come the succession of revolutions and the hatred of black and white which to this day has kept Haiti in the rearguard of civilization.

The era of the French revolution gave an

opening for the first negro rebellion, and led by the example of the white planters who rebelled against their own government, the mulattoes organized to some extent and a man named Oge attempted to obtain justice in both Paris and from the local authorities. Failing, he was sought as a rebel and after armed resistance by himself and his followers he was captured and executed.

Critical conditions soon led the French Constituent Assembly to send three Commissioners from France to restore order and also issued a decree that "every man of color, born of free parents should enjoy equal political rights with the whites." However, the feeling in Haiti was so strong against this act that pressure was brought to bear upon Governor Blanchelande which prevented his executing the decree and pitched battles took place between the whites and the blacks.

The French Government, largely through

incapable Commissioners whom they had sent, was losing her grip on the control of Haitian affairs, and at the same time there arose two contending forces to control affairs there. In the north the negros had succeeded in becoming the stronger factor and a slave, named Toussaint L'Overture, though at first faithful to his master, soon saw the inevitable trend of affairs and joined the rebels. He very quickly proved his ability for leadership and was soon chosen their chief.

In the meanwhile the English had, with a ridiculously small force, taken St. Marc and afterwards Port-au-Prince. After Toussaint had firmly established himself in the north, he marched southward to essay the attacking of the English. Time after time he attempted to force them to surrender, but each effort was repulsed. Soon, however, the English realized the impossibility of conquering Haiti, and decided to evacuate. They treated with Toussaint and left St. Marc and Port-au-Prince to him and his party of the north.

At this point Toussaint showed his discerning insight into the entire black versus white situation at that time by allowing all foreigners who sided with him to remain undisturbed in the newly-acquired territory. But this action did not meet with favor from all, and, chiefly through the influence of Hedouville, many whites were murdered contrary to the order of Toussaint.

Rigoud, in control of the south, now opposed Toussaint but was forced to make peace with him when the French sent a commission and supported Toussaint's claim to rule. Among the generals of Toussaint was Dessalines who commanded his troops in the north while Toussaint was himself in the vicinity of Port-au-Prince. Dessalines, like Hedouville, was radically opposed to the equality policy of Toussaint and while the latter was away he

CIVIL PRISONERS AT PORT-AU-PRINCE MAKING CHAIRS

was intolerant of the mulattos and murdered thousands of them.

Toussaint, in spite of these disagreements and violations of his orders, was nevertheless supreme in Haiti. He now aspired to the throne of Santo Domingo as well. Therefore, all preparations completed, he set out upon his new march of conquest and, not meeting a single reverse, Toussaint, upon his return, claimed possession of the entire island.

But here Toussaint made his fatal step. Instead of declaring the independence of Haiti he ruled it as a French colony with himself as the self-appointed governor and with his creed based upon equality for white, black and mulatto. The result of this policy was that when France was again at peace, Bonaparte was able to make an attempt to again bring Haiti back to the condition of slavery. By false trickery the French General Leclerc captured Toussaint and exiled him to the Alps, where he soon died. Toussaint, the conqueror, thus lost his chance of becoming Toussaint, the founder of the republic.

War was now declared between France and England and opportunity again arose for the French to be driven from Haiti. Dessalines with many of Toussaint's former generals accomplished this task and declared the country independent. Dessalines was made Governor-General and declared the "Founder of Haitian Independence." He is known everywhere under this title to-day, and is far more revered than Toussaint as the great national hero. Inspired by the crowning of Bonaparte in 1804, Dessalines declared himself the first emperor of Haiti and from that time on until his death he continued to rule a one-man power of terrorism and brutality.

Upon the death of Dessalines, rival claims were made by the various sectional chiefs for the crown of the new Haitian Empire. Out of these leaders Christophe arose in the north as the strongest contender and after proclaiming himself King Henry I of Haiti, he succeeded in practically eliminating all other leaders except Petion who was very powerful in the south. But these two rivals were forced to unite their forces and strength in common cause against the French who made a new but unfruitful effort to regain possession of the island.

Petion and Christophe were opposite types. Petion was rather easy-going and it was this which held his followers to him rather than any show of force. But Christophe, second only to Dessalines as a national hero, was even more despotic than that emperor in the treatment of his own people.

It was Christophe who built the great citadel at Cap Haitien and who, taking his architect up to show him the view from the cliff, pitched him into eternity lest he might disclose his knowledge of the secret passages which he had designed. In building the Citadel, the ascent was so steep as to make almost beyond the limits of human endurance the carrying up of heavy building materials. It is said that the 5000 men assigned to do this work refused, and, upon hearing of this, Christophe had the men lined up and every other man killed. He then commanded the remaining 2500 to complete the task or they should receive the same fate as the others.

But this iron rule of Christophe proved to be a boomerang for him and a man named Boyer, who was by this time the leader in the south, marched northward and declared Haiti a republic and himself its first president. The north was tired of Christophe and willingly joined in with the cause of Boyer. Under Boyer, Santo Domingo declared herself independent and in allegiance to President Boyer of Haiti, who thus became chief of the entire island.

The next event was the demand by France for indemnity and Boyer acceded to this demand on condition that France sign a treaty acknowledging the independence of Haiti. This was agreed to and two treaties were signed, but the indemnity always remained practically unpaid, for revolution after revolution made a collection of the indemnity through a blockade impossible.

After the death of Boyer, strong rule was lacking for a long time and the government was ever-changing, being overthrown by each succeeding revolution. This was largely due to the fact that there was no ruler who was acceptable to both the blacks and the mulattoes, who were now the two constantly opposed factors. It is said that the Haitian flag of red and blue was formed from the French by eliminating the white even as the white race had been eliminated from the island, and leaving only the blue for the blacks and the red for the mullatoes. Nevertheless it is certain that these two remaining colors could not live in harmony together. No rule was long stable and frequent and serious uprisings which resulted in interference with the foreigners in Haiti caused the diplomatic corps many a critical problem. Law and order were unknown and few were the presidents of that period who died a natural death.

Finally, in 1915, the climax came. President Sam was driven from his palace by the mob, and chased by them through the streets. Finally they followed him when he sought refuge in the French territory of the legation and he was there massacred and cut to shreds before the eyes of the wife and children of the French minister. Intervention by the French was naturally imminent, but in order to preserve the integrity of the Monroe Doctrine, America took the lead and forced the existing government of Haiti to accept a treaty which temporarily allows America a sufficiently free hand in Haiti to maintain law and order and to help the Haitians build up a civilized and stable government.

And so it is that we are to-day visiting Haiti and that it is now possible to travel in a country which was previously in the throes of continual unrest. Whereas before the Occupation, practically no administration was able to complete its term of office, foreign business was unable to hazard investments and personal safety was uncertain; protection is now afforded to the foreigner who comes to Haiti, and equality of treatment in public for all colors is the rule.

IV

VAUDOUX

HAITI is one of the few countries where State and Church still remain united, and to-day the Catholic clergy are under government pay. Roman Catholicism first became the Haitian religion when, in 1836, the Pope was declared its head and given the authority to appoint its bishops. The priests are almost uniformly upright men who are working along beneficial lines among the natives and are one of the leading forces for good in the country.

The masses in Haiti, however, do not believe in straight Catholicism but in Vaudouxism. This creed is of African origin and was introduced into Haiti when the black slaves were brought over by the Spanish and French. To

WOMEN CARRYING IN TO MARKET BASKETS WHICH THEY
HAVE MADE. LIKE EVERYTHING ELSE THEY ARE CARRIED
ON THEIR HEADS

THE CATHEDRAL

these original beliefs they have slowly accumulated a few Indian superstitions and very many of the ceremonies and attributes of Christianity, so that Vaudouxism as it exists in Haiti to-day is a unique religion.

Vaudoux is the deity of the Vaudouxists and is represented as a venomless serpent. The human leader of the creed is a high priest selected by the followers of Vaudoux from among themselves and is known as Papaloi, and he in turn selects a high priestess who is called Mamanloi (corruptions of the words Papa Roi and Maman Roi). In these two personages is supposed to be the divine spark. But, mixed with this pure Vaudouxism, there is much Christian ceremony, such as the inclusion of the worship of the Virgin Mary and the observance of Easter Day.

Like all primitive religious cults, the Vaudouxists include in their rites sacrifices and self-inflicted punishments. Animals of various kinds are sacrificed at each meeting of Vaudouxists and the highest offering is the snow-white sacred goat. To the rhythm of Vaudoux drums or tom-toms, the worshippers dance themselves into excited passions for hour after hour, until the chief dancers, who alone remain, finally fall from utter exhaustion. During this dance the men eat pieces of glass and, dancing upon red-hot coals, they place burning pieces of charcoal in their mouth. And we read of the asce ticism of the Middle Ages and think of it as a bygone phrase!

Often at the Vaudoux meetings the participants become maddened by the liquor and revel, and debauchery finally prevails in its lowest forms, until the meeting breaks up at dawn. But the endurance of the chief dancers who continue for five, six and seven hours without ceasing for a moment, is truly marvelous.

So great is the fear of Vaudoux inbred in the Haitian that even with those who are civilized and cultured, many remain in awe of Vaudoux or are restrained from exerting their influence against it through fear of poisoning, for the Haitians are arch-poisoners. And thus, though many Haitians of the upper classes are nominally good Catholics, they are still to a more or less extent subservient to Vaudoux superstitions and avoid openly opposing the demonstrations of it by their countrymen.

Many of the presidents of Haiti were themselves Vaudoux priests and but two among them took any active measures toward repressing it. These two were Geffrard and Boisson-Canal and the act meant their downfall, for Vaudouxism is habitually aided or winked at by the Government. Toussaint L'Overture was an out-and-out Catholic and took definite measures against Vaudouxism, but in his day the beliefs were not so strong and it was much easier to repress its practice.

It is now impossible for the Vaudouxists to
openly hold their meetings near the towns and
they are forced to find some rendezvous among
the hills. But in the towns the natives still
hold their dances, where they dance the weird
"bambeula" to the beat of the tom-tom very
much as they do at the real Vaudoux meetings.
The tom-toms are made out of a hollow log and
two skins which are made taut over each end of
the log. The tom-tom beater is skilled and as
particular about his instrument and how it is
tuned up (by tightening or loosening the bind-
ings of the skins) as any violinist. The tom-
tom beater knows many different native tunes.

And so Vaudouxism still prevails the driv-
ing religious force of most Haitians. The
most uncivilized are out-and-out worshippers
and regularly attend the Vaudoux rendezvous,
but the higher classes are ashamed to confess
their subservience to Vaudouxism to foreigners and consequently many pose as Catholics

although sometimes they are themselves Papalois. And then there are those Haitians who are truly Catholics, and these are in most cases those who have been educated abroad. They are usually of the younger generation. But as I have shown they dislike intensely to come out openly against the practice of Vaudouxism by other Haitians.

The elimination of Vaudouxism, in fact, rests almost entirely upon the shoulders of the Americans. And this elimination is imperative for Vaudouxism is, not so much a religious evil, but an unmoral and uncivilizing factor. It is Vaudouxism, too, which makes more difficult the fighting of the cacos; for Vaudoux priests have, through their hold upon the religious fear of the Vaudouxists, tremendous power over all their doings. Upon the sounding of a Vaudoux drum the priest can very often do about what he wants with his followers. Probably all of the caco chiefs are Vaudoux priests and thus hold together bands which, freed from religious scruples, would abandon their purpose of brigandry. For example, in the January raid, many of the cacos who had been wounded, admitted that they had gone into the attack only because of their belief that the Vaudoux charms which they wore made them invulnerable.

One Sunday while I was waiting at the Gendarme headquarters at Leogane there was being held there the weekly meeting of the "Communale" and the Gendarme officer told me that the chief of this force was one of the natives who had always joined in every revolution which had reached that part of the country and the third chief was formerly an ally of the great caco leader, Charlemagne. A strange band, certainly, to be the guardians of law and order. But it was, after all, reasonable. These men were the most intelligent in their neighborhood and then of course it was infinitely better to have such men in a place where their salaries would keep them law-abiding than to have them outside the law and inciting trouble against a less capable government force.

It is very difficult to establish any sort of efficient and just civil force because of the ignorance of the vast majority of the Haitian population. The number of intelligent, or partly intelligent men in a country district is small, and it is the intelligent men in these sections who are usually in league with the cacos, either openly or secretly. And with the magistrates there is another obstacle which prevents the execution of justice. Ever since the beginnings of Haitian history, graft has been so natural and accepted a thing with government officials that it is inborn in the present generation and time alone will ever wipe it out.

At present with a large number of the magistrates impartial judgment is unknown and the local law verdict goes to the highest bidder. First one side buys up the judge and then the other until finally one party is forced to give in through lack of resources. The chief drawback in attempting to eliminate such graft is the ridiculously low pay given to a magistrar. It is but natural for a judge to seek outside gains in order that he may earn a living. When a Haitian dies, and some of the more prosperous of them have accumulated fortunes of over a hundred thousand dollars, the heirs or even outsiders who are on the spot loot his wealth and leave nothing for any absent members of the family. The latter are unable to obtain justice later because the first-comers have carefully bought up the local officials with a portion of their new gains.

This unfair state of local government can be remedied only slowly and by the gradual elimination of the idea of graft as an expected

A SOURCE OF THE GREATEST GOOD—THE ROMAN CATHOLIC
SISTERS AT ONE OF THE MANY CONVENTS ON THE ISLAND

THE HEAD NURSE AT THE PUBLIC HOSPITAL WITH HER CORPS
OF HAITIAN NURSES

right of a government official. But as I have
pointed out the raising of the magistrate's salary is a prerequisite. The low salary now
paid is of course due to the lack of funds which
hinders the development of the country at
every turn.

Under the provisions of the American
treaty with Haiti, the entire financial situation
was placed, during the duration of the treaty,
in the hands of a financial advisor, who, having
been nominated by the President of the United
States, is appointed by the President of Haiti.
Addison P. Ruan was the first appointee and
served in Haiti for two years until he was
transferred to take the same post in Panama.
Following Mr. Ruan, John A. McIlhenny
came to Haiti and, realizing like his predeces-
sor the urgent need for money with which to
develop the country, he has been steadily at
work to put through a Haitian loan in the

United States. This is of course at present impossible due to the abnormal financial situation in this country.

The financial advisor in Haiti has the authority to make all appropriations of the state money and his word is final as to their expenditure. In this respect Haiti is being run, during the treaty period, in very much the same way as India is governed by England, except that no treasurer is needed in Haiti, as the Haitian National Bank serves that purpose.

V

PUBLIC EDUCATION AND NORMIL CHARLES

M DANTES BELLEGARDE, Minister of Public Instruction, had told us that he would be glad to show us through the schools of Port-au-Prince. We therefore arranged a date and set out one morning to make the tour. With us went also the American Advisor to the department, Mr. Bourgeois.

At the time the treaty was made between Haiti and the United States, no provision was arranged for the Department of Education, as was done with the Sanitary and Engineering Departments. Thus the development made possible through the more direct assistance from Washington has been unattainable in the school work, and although the work we saw being carried on was a remarkably inspiring demonstration of accomplishments, yet the small proportion which is being done of what could be done if greater means were available is quite discouraging. It is the same cry as one raises on every hand: If only they had the means!

Two years ago, three years after the treaty was signed, Mr. Bourgeois came to Haiti, but only in the capacity of an Advisor responsible to the Haitian Government alone and not as a league official. His force is largely restricted to negative powers.

It is indeed fortunate that a mind of remarkable keenness and a power for practical work exists in the person of the present Minister, M. Bellegarde. But should a man of lesser force take his place, as has happened within recent years, the result would be deplorable. Also, M. Bellegarde could carry his work much further if he had the proper financial and other material aid of the United States Educational Department.

Although compulsory educations is legally a fact, there is, in reality, a force of teachers and equipment for but 18,000 of the 200,000 children of the proper age. Many of these children are in the country districts where good teachers, who even in the city are at a premium, are almost an unknown factor. This feature is being remedied as far as practicable, all the time, and the teachers in the rural schools are being carefully examined. Some of these have been found to be utterly unable to correct their pupils' simple exercises and these teachers are being dropped. But, though it is thus very simple to drop an incompetent teacher, it is a manifold more difficult task to replace him. The pay for teachers is $6 per month and so, even low as wages are in Haiti, the position of teacher is not so lucrative as to have very many applicants.

The salaries cannot be raised. It is the old story of lack of money. Nearly half of the annual appropriation for public instruction is being swallowed up by the present salaries of the present number of teachers. The remainder is naturally barely sufficient to maintain the existing schools. No new advances are possible.

Fortunately, besides the public schools of Haiti, there are numerous privately run ones, nearly always under religious or parti-religious supervision. The Catholics are the most frequent benefactors and are doing by far the greater part of the work. Originally, before the present public school system was created, these schools, missions, or convents were in part supported by the state; but gradually this assistance is being necessarily taken away.

Our first visit was to a school run by Belgian Sisters. It was a school for girls only and was still supported in part by the Government.

For the younger children the work consists mostly of such studies as would be taught in a primary school in the States, great stress being laid upon the speaking of good French. This is particularly important because the natural tongue of the lower classes of natives is Creole, which in Haiti consists of an ungrammatical and corrupted language drawn principally from the French, but also with traces of English, Spanish and early Indian words. Some Creole words seem to defy a tracing of their origin. Although the natives may understand you if you speak French to them, it is impossible for you to make out what they say, though you may know French perfectly.

"Vini non" is a Creole expression used continually to mean "come here!" Its derivation is certainly obscure. Nor is Creole the same all over the republic. Each section has its own dialect which is distinct.

After the children learn the first elements

of grammar school work, they begin to work a part of the day at embroidery, sewing and knitting. Thus the vocational work is gradually increased and before the girls graduate they are given training which fits them to be efficient servants. Vocational schools of this type are just what Haiti needs most of all. They serve the double purpose of training the natives to obtain a good living and they also furnish a means by which the better-off may secure good servants and workers.

Downstairs in the school building are the school and work rooms—upstairs the dormitory. The dormitory consists of one large room covering the entire top of the house and filled with cots for every boarder. For every two cots there is also provided a washstand which contains places where they may keep their personal articles. The entire effect was of an establishment thoroughly modern and scrupulously clean. Besides these girls who

MAGISTRAR'S STAND—OF WHICH THERE IS ONE IN EVERY
TOWN

THE NEW PRESIDENT'S PALACE

come from the country districts and board, the school has also a great many day pupils who live at their homes in town.

The next school we went to was a non-vocational one under the direction of an order of French Brothers. It was solely for boys, just as the first was only a girls' school, for the morals of the country do not permit the adoption of co-education, even though the pupils are of the earliest ages.

The priests who conduct this institution are certainly as fine a type of self-sacrificing men who are aiding a truly worthy cause as I can imagine. They see the tremendous possibilities and without limiting their efforts to what they could accomplish with a normal amount of work they undertake almost superhuman attempts. Of the Brothers who come to Haiti, their average length of life after arriving is but 12 years, so killing is their work. The normal amount of work for a professor in the United States is about 18 hours a week, but the Brothers in Haiti teach for 8 hours every single day. And every effort which they put into it is unwasted and has a telling effect in the result.

There are 11 grades of scholars taught by the Brothers, from the earliest kindergarten to the graduation class who would correspond to high school students. The boys are given work in geography, history, spelling, French, mathematics and other things which would be taught in any American school. I looked over the copy books of the younger boys and the neatness and excellent penmanship of even children of six was amazing. All of the children seemed to be naturally gifted at freehand drawing. One little boy of eight, when asked what his favorite subject was, replied: "My national emblem." He drew therewith a fine representation of a palm tree.

Although the order of Brothers is French, not all of them are Frenchmen. Several are Americans, a few Canadians and Portuguese, and one, a Haitian Brother.

Our third and last visit was to the Ecôle Normale d'Industrie. The graduating pupils here act as teachers of the younger ones. This school is one of the public schools and as we went through it, M. Bellegarde proudly pointed to a particularly fine-looking little boy. "That is my son." We went through many classrooms full of scholars of different ages studying in very much the same way as children study in America. It seemed a cause for hope to look at this public school through which the Haitian children were being made to see the advantages of education and the opportunity to rise. When every Haitian child will be able to have such instruction and training then his genration will be able to throw off the yoke of past superstitions and dispel the ignorance which has been holding back the masses.

Following this tour of the few schools which time allowed us to visit, M. Bellegarde took us to the studio of Normil Charles. M. Charles is a Haitian sculptor who has remarkable genius and is one of the leading sculptors of the world. He studied in Paris for a number of years, and has received many decorations and honors. As we entered his studio, in front of us we saw a huge bronze which he is doing for the Government and which is to be placed in the Champ de Mars. It is called "The Benefactor" and is the statue of a great public-spirited man. At his feet kneels a peasant woman, with babe in arms, mourning his death. The piece would certainly be a work of the first class anywhere and the country may well be proud that one of its citizens is its author.

In the studio, too, was the bust of Dessalines,

done by Charles, and which I had seen six months before in the Pan-American Building in Washington, where it remained for some time.

M. Charles, himself, is a delightful man, well-mannered and interesting. But he is indeed a strange product of a country which for so many years has been kept down by revolution with the resulting isolation and lack of opportunity to devote time to the pursuits of peace.

VI

FROM the studio of M. Charles, M. Bellegarde took us to see the new palace. It is a huge structure, quite like a palace in appearance, and made of white stucco. It is more than twice the size of our White House and is shaped like the letter E, with the three wings running back from the front. In the main hall huge columns rise to the ceiling and at each side a staircase winds up to the second floor.

While we were starting to go through the palace the guard had apprised President Dartiguenave of our presence and we were surprised and delighted to have him send word that he would be glad to receive us. Although the left wing of the building is to be the Presi-

dent's private suite, it is as yet uncompleted
and he is at present occupying the opposite
end. We entered the President's office, where
he rose from his desk to meet us, and to usher
us through to the Cabinet room. This room
is large, like all the rooms—perhaps 40 feet
square—and with a long table in the center
surrounded by chairs. Here the President
meets his Cabinet.

The President is a man of medium height
and has the bearing of an aristocrat. His
hair and beard are gray which contribute to
his good appearance. He is rather light in
color and, indeed, is the first president for a
long time who has not been a black. The
President does not speak English but under-
stands and speaks French perfectly. Al-
together he is a delightful, cultured man and
a suitable head for the Republic.

From the balcony of the palace there is an
excellent view, overlooking the entire town and

the harbor beyond. The next room to visit was the "Salle Diplomatique" where all official receptions are held. This had just been decorated but was as yet unfinished. The President personally escorted us to it and afterwards to his future private suite. He then showed us downstairs and out to the car, where we left both the President and M. Bellegarde.

"WHITE WINGS" OF PORT-AU-PRINCE

MARKET WOMEN LEAVING TOWN ON THEIR "BURROS"

VII

A MORNING HUNT

AS I left the house one morning at two, the yard boys next door were already at work and in town the "white wings" —an American institution—were about. Three of us joggled along for 22 miles for an early duck shoot and talked of many things, among them concerning a proposed map of Haiti. The existing one is grossly inaccurate as is easily shown by an airplane flight or a ship attempting to follow many of the channels. There is no triangulation point in Haiti and so the present coast line on the maps is the result of a certain number of bearings from off shore, with the remainder a matter of free-hand filling-in. The use of airplanes in heretofore untried ways will be employed to aid in the exact location of towns and be a means of a great saving of tedious traverse work.

In town, life was already stirring, as I have shown. This is nothing unusual for it is the customary hour for the Haitian to begin his day. By 6 the "gentlemen about town" are in the streets with their canes and Stetsons, debating the fall of the cabinet or the latest development in the gourde situation. But out in the country everything was still dark and the market women had barely started to bring their load into town. So we met no one—except twice the marine patrol car on its route.

Just outside the portals marking the limits of Port-au-Prince on which are inscribed the words: "Peace, Justice, Work," is the historic Pont Rouge. This is the spot where revolutionary troops coming down from the mountains and across the plains would first meet the forces of the existing government of Port-au-Prince. Here the great Dessalines, com-

ing into town at the head of his troops, met
what he believed to be a guard of his own
troops. His own general was leading them,
but had betrayed Dessalines, and the President
was soon left wounded in the roadway to die.
It had been Dessalines who, it is said, sported
himself by pulling out the eyes of his prisoners
with corkscrews.

The streets in Port-au-Prince are wide as-
phalt pavements and would be adapted for
speeding but for the presence in the center and
sides promiscuously of unruly "burros," naked
babies playing in the dirt, odd Haitian pigs
looking like some new species of animal, and
pedestrians of strange sorts. This is true,
also, for some distance out on the Hasco road,
over which we went. But after a few miles
we came out upon one of the new roads which
has been put down throughout the island by
the Haitian Government under the supervision
of the Gendarmerie and of an engineering

force loaned to them by the United States. In all, about 500 miles of excellent roadways have been put down since the American intervention.

In this work the budget system is now used and as every payment is actually handed out by one of the American engineers himself, the graft which was formerly rampant has been eliminated. In the days of pre-American intervention a sum of, let us assume, $50,000 was voted to build a road. $5,000 of this regularly went to the President and $500 to each Senator who would vote for the appropriation. This left, generally, about $10,000, or one-fifth, for actual road building work.

The Haitians have proven to be good engineers and except for the pay roll, large pieces of work are often carried on by them without assistance from the Americans.

The first part of the road which we struck was excellent but after branching off the main road to Pont Beudet we came to the new part. Roads of this type, which is the one generally used, are macadam with good foundation of different sized stones and 20 feet in width. The top dressing is a good binding gravel which can be found within short distances along almost all of the roads which they are now building. A temporary track is run from each gravel pit along the side of the road until a mile or so on another pit is dug and the rails taken up and laid down from the new pit on. The gravel is thus carried to where it is needed by a small engine and a few cars. There is in this way no long-distance hauling.

Finally we turned off the new road to a clearing through a cactus desert at the edge of Lake Troucaiman. Above either shore two mountain ranges run parallel for miles, far above the lake. The lake itself is open water in the central portion but by far the greater part is filled with a mass of lily, mangrove and reed growth. Often it is so dense as to be entirely impenetrable.

When we arrived at Troucaiman it was not yet daylight and only the candles in the few "cailles" along the road could be seen. Upon the approach of the car, five or six natives appeared, knowing from past experience what we had come for, and with our French and their Creole, interspersed by numerous gestures, we made our plans. Each of us started out, alone in his own tiny dugout of about a foot wide and four feet long and with his own native in the back to pole him about. The guides had taken off the few rags which they wore and one by one we were shoved off. Part of the time we were poled, part of the time the craft stuck and the native had to wade along beside to keep us going.

We went on and on in the blackness until finally one could distinguish black shapes arising from the water or whirring past. It came at last—the gray dawn for which we had been waiting. A teal went overhead with its characteristic rapid flight. A slower-flying redhead and later a scaup passed. And all around were hundreds upon hundreds of Egrets, great white forms which flappingly arose when we approached too near.

To the natives there are four kinds of ducks: "gens-gens," which is a species of tree duck; "cécele" or blue-winged teal; "cucurem" or ruddy duck; and any other duck is known as "canard generale." All of the first three species are abundant, as are also the scaup, baldpate, redhead and Bahaman pintail.

We met at nine on the shore, which by daylight looked very different than when we had left it, and after some refreshments and comparing of our respective bags, we started home. There are no game laws in Haiti, so that your bag is only limited by your lack of skill. Half way in to Port-au-Prince is the spot where two

months before three Haitian engineers had
been murdered in the "caille" where they were
spending the night. The men were working
on the road I have spoken of, but as the caco
trouble had been active in that district just
before the men were murdered, these men had
been duly forewarned not to spend the night.

Frequently I used to go out on these shooting trips, but not always to Troucaiman. Two
other spots were alternated, Miragôane in the
west and the salt lakes beyond Troucaiman.
These salt lakes are two decidedly brackish
bodies of water which lie on the border of Haiti
and Santo Domingo. They are at the end
of the Plain of the Cul-de-Sac, and a few miles
beyond the town of Thomaseau. The water
is as clear as a crystal and the scenery amid
these wonderful lakes and the mountains above
them is splendid.

In the opposite direction, and 70 miles west
of Port-au-Prince, is Lake Miragôane. It is

TYPICAL "CAILLE" NEAR FURCY

A few banana and coffee trees (on the left) are all that each one has

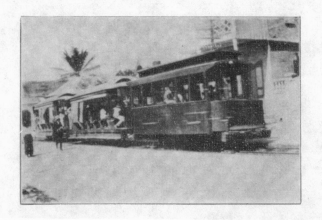

RAILWAY TO LEOGANE

just beyond Petit Gôave. The lake is large, being about eight miles long. In a part of the lake we had particularly good teal shooting and by moonlight thousands of "gens-gens" would come in to feed in the shallows overnight. Long before dawn they had vanished again.

It is a difficult lake to shoot upon, however. The mud flats from the shore are long and reach far out into the lake so that it is practically impossible to use a dugout for some distance. Thus it was necessary to walk out in shallow water and deep mud. The water, very unlike the salt lake water, was thick, filthy and always gave one an itching sensation for hours after having been in it.

Beside the duck shooting at Miragôane, there is excellent snipe shooting during certain seasons and good guinea shooting also. It is a strange thing to have guineas in Haiti. The guinea is a native of Africa which only reached the new world in a domesticated state.

The present birds are descendants of the domesticated ones left by the French planters during the revolution and which have reverted to the wild state in the intervening generations. Doves, as everywhere in Haiti are also abundant, and form a good shoot and a good meal.

VIII

PINE NEEDLES

THE mountains had changed from green to violet and from violet to black and the new moon silhouetted the peaks from 10,000 foot summits to the sea. From Furcy, the next range to the east seemed within hands' reach across the valleys and hills as its mountains rose ten miles or ten hours by trail away. Our sweaters and blankets felt barely enough as the wind howled around us. With closed eyes we knew from its tell-tale sound that pine trees surrounded us and that the winds were blowing stronger and stronger through their needles.

We climbed the hill with difficulty over the slippery matting of pine needles to pick bananas along the road. And we were in the tropics, with pine cones, palm and bananas growing side by side. Thanking Providence that I am alive while such country still exists, untouched by man's civilization, I gazed for dozens of miles over several mountain ranges with their valleys and hills overlapping to the sea on two sides of the island. These bits of water looked far away indeed.

With only a rough, mountain-stream bed winding for miles to the nearest town, we were apart by so much from white man—but in point of effect upon the country as far as before Columbus saw the first redskin when he landed on the north shore of the island.

Tucked away in the valleys we could see the lights of many native "cailles" and we knew that there were many more unseen. With plaster and sticks for walls they are roofed by thatching of straw overhanging the walls and sloping up to a peak. In every part of Haiti they are there, each the same with its 2 or 3 coffee trees, its few bananas and that is about all. Along the road are the market women. Every so often, perhaps once a week, they take their bananas or coffee to town, a walk for some of 18 hours' steady going, to sell it at the Port-au-Prince market for about 50 cents gold.

And the natives are satisfied—in fact they do not want things to be any different. They have enough to live on and have no desires which more energy would gratify. For amusement they have their cock fights, when all the neighborhood gathers and each man brings his trained rooster. And in the evenings they have their native dances with tom-tom music and native rum, *taffia, clairin* and *rum,* the first entirely unrefined, the second somewhat refined, and the third refined, though very often not of an excellent grade. But some Haitian rum can be easily obtained which is excellent and of just about as good quality as Jamaica rum.

And then, of course, besides the bananas and coffee which they sell, the natives in the hills burn charcoal and carry this, whenever they need money, to town for 60 cts. a donkey load.

We had left Port-au-Prince in the morning by car to Petionville, 1200 feet above the sea, and from there had changed to horseback. With our pack-mules and gendarme guides we left Petionville at noon and started the winding trail up the first mountain range. The going was slow as the trail is mostly steep and in places merely a stream-bed filled with loose rocks. Within the first hour we were far up and could look upon Petionville just below us and beyond it the broad plain of the Cul-de-Sac with its many squares of bright green sugar cane cut in the brown-gray cactus

land. As a background for this flat valley
rose the mountains of Mirebalais continuing
beyond the ends of the plain to the sea and to
the salt lakes. Just this side of the salt lakes
was a mass of water and reeds, looking very
insignificant, which was the familiar Troucaiman. It was like an aërial photograph of this
entire section of the country but with perspec-
tive and magnificently varied coloration.

And so we went on over the second range
to get our first glimpse of Kenskoff—a tiny
mountain village half-way up the third mountain slope. We climbed up the winding trails
which sometimes consisted of cuts through the
mountains, but generally paths cut in the
mountainside, with the crest high above us and
the base far below. At Kenskoff is a tiny white
chapel with the Pope's flag of white and yellow
marking it from a long distance. This out-
post of Christianity is visited perhaps once a

month by the priest of the neighborhood on his rounds.

After watering our horses and having a few eggs and sandwiches, we left Kenskoff and the mountains became more barren. A red-tailed hawk soared in the valley below us and from the roadside we flushed flocks of mourning dove at every curve. And then we reached Furcy, and around the side of the mountain we suddenly came upon the entire panorama of each succeeding range rolling up from the distant ones, which were in Santo Domingo, to drop from 10,000 feet to the valley below us and rise again to our pathway of about one mile high.

It was a clear night with a new moon, so only a few tiny clouds floated below us in the valleys and above only the black and gold of a starlit night.

ON THE ST. MARC ROAD AFTER THE HEAVY RAINS

IX

COTTON

THE week before Christmas we started off on a motor trip as the guests of Mr. and Mrs. H. P. Davis. Mr. Davis is the Vice-President of the United West Indies Corporation, an American concern which is engaged in developing the resources of Haiti. Although operating throughout the Republic, the largest plantation of the company is near St. Michel in the north-central portion, where for miles the country is a vast fertile plain and thus peculiarly valuable as agricultural land. The soil is virgin—untouched and unused except in the early Spanish days, centuries ago, for cattle grazing. That part of Haiti near and to the westward of St. Michel was never in the possession of the

French as was the rest of the Republic, but was held by the Spanish until driven back to the present Dominican border by the Haitians themselves.

The first day's ride of about seven hours brought us to St. Michel. The route from Port-au-Prince for two-thirds of the way is along the bay to Gonaïves. From there the road goes directly inland. The country through which one passes during these hours contains many changes, for from the fertile plains outside of Port-au-Prince, where castor bean and sugar cane are growing, there is suddenly a cessation of verdant growth beyond St. Marc, and for miles a near-desert stretches out. The road is merely a clearing of the cactus growth which closes in on either side and consists of queer-looking species of cacti. The soil is sandy, the air humid, and the thorny mass on every side impenetrable. Every now and then we would pass partly wild mules kicking down the trunk of a cactus to drink the water it contained; and as we pased, some of the natives would rush madly into the bushes from fright. It is not so long since they saw their first motor and they are still filled with fear when one appears.

From the plains of Dessalines, a few miles south of Gonaïves, there is an excellent view of the three old Haitian forts in the mountains back of the plain. Here the Haitiens retreated to wait until the forces should come across the plains to attack them. It is easy to see how difficult it was for any force to attempt to attack the Haitians when once intrenched in their forts, situated on cliffs and with hidden trails leading to them.

Stopping for a moment in the plains, we saw a woman coming up to the car. We found out that she wished to sell her baby if she could get a few gourdes (20-cent pieces of our money but corresponding in Haiti to a dollar) for it. Again at Gonaïves a small boy begged us to take him home and keep him, in exchange for which he would do any work we might wish. This sort of temporary slavery which many children enter into or are sold into by their parents lasts generally until they are of age, during which time they do any work which you may assign them to. It is a common custom.

From Gonaïves the road to St. Michel passes through Ennery and it was on the outskirts of this town that we stopped for luncheon. The spot was a clearing in a forest with huge ancient trees and little coffee bushes surrounding. In the clearing were the stone pillars, some still erect, some fallen, of what was once the palace of Toussaint L'Overture.

Beyond Ennery there is a stiff climb for a number of miles until finally one comes out on the plateau which constitutes the plains of St. Michel. Passing through the town, which is at the southern end of the plain of Atalaye, we went a short distance before arriving at the headquarters of the plantation. Here we spent the night. The main building is a very attractive structure, all the rooms of which except the kitchen and office being on the second floor. All around is a second-story veranda supported by wooden posts from below. We sat late watching the headlights of the tractors moving about ceaselessly over the plains.

The next day was spent in looking over the plantation and seeing the new long staple cotton which they are growing in large quantities. Also, in the afternoon we had a long ride across the plains and afterward a guinea and dove shoot.

At 6 on the morning of the second day we started out in our car for Cap Haitien. After passing Ennery the road begins to climb up and up, gaining the steep ascent only by curving and recurving along the side of each mountain slope. The range was the Puilboreaux Mountains which climatically divide the island into the north and south. In Port-au-Prince and all of southern Haiti we were in the middle of the dry season, as I have said. But after we were over the summit of Puilboreaux all was changed. The foliage, which on the southern slope was dry, was now verdant and profuse, the road muddy instead of dusty and everywhere flowers of all kinds flourished. Each woods had the orchids out in bloom.

Once over the top of Puilboreau, the view is wonderful. Mountains miles away look very near and just below it seems, though it is really far, lies the valley of Plaisance with the little white buildings of the town tucked away in the center.

Before reaching the Cap, as Cap Haitian is called throughout Haiti, it is necessary to ford the Limbé River. Normally this is very simple and a motor will cross over without any trouble. Sometimes, however, in the floods of the rainy season it becomes impassable and crossing is impossible for days at a time. When we arrived it was doubtful, but we were informed that with the aid of the prisoners in the gendarme prison there, it would be possible. We started, pulled by a rope, pushed by forty black figures with rags to indicate the prison cloth, out into midstream under the direction of a gendarme. But half way out we stuck, the car filled with water to the seats and only after everyone was up to his neck in water beside the car helping to push it, did we finally arrive on the other side.

Cap Haitien is to-day not a very important town, compared to Port-au-Prince, but it was the capital in the French days, and the center of a large amount of commerce. It shows, unlike other towns, decided traces of the Spanish architecture. The harbor is beautiful and along the side there runs a drive to the eastward.

The great sight of the north I did not see. It is the Citadel and Sans Souci, the palace of Christophe. In the mountains far above the Cap the Citadel lay surrounded by mist except for a few minutes early the next morning, when the clouds were swept away and we got one glimpse of the Citadel. But we were unable to take the trail which winds up to the palace and the Citadel because of the heavy rains which at that time flooded the region.

HAITIAN WOMEN WASHING THEIR CLOTHES IN A DITCH

THE AMERICAN CLUB

X

THE blood of the present-day Haitian is largely a mixture of French and black. The Indian aborigines were totally eliminated from Haiti by the Spaniard, so that unlike the most of Latin America, the Indians or their descendants form no part of the population. The Spaniard, in turn, was driven from Haiti by the French before he had left much of an imprint and his blood forms a negligible factor to-day. The English, although in Haiti, were there so short a time as to leave no strain of British blood. And so the French blood is predominant.

Also, all the closest connections of Haiti are still with France, or were up to the time of the American Occupation. Creole is based more fundamentally upon French than any other language and the conversation of the higher classes is pure French. Many Haitians go each year to Paris to study or to visit, and many of the most prominent are educated there.

When the Americans took the leading rôle in Haiti there naturally arose with greater force the race question. The feeling between black and white is so much stronger between most Americans and the black races than it is in the case of Europeans, that it becomes a serious problem. It is foolishly intolerant of the American who goes to Haiti to assume an attitude of mental or social superiority over the Haitian because he is a black. It would be equally absurd for the Haitian to attempt to break through the walls of prejudice and to expect all Americans and Haitians to mix with ease. Although it is most certainly true that America has an infinitely more thorough knowledge and is more capable of government than is Haiti, yet the Haitians have what many Americans of even the upper classes often lack, a knowledge of culture and excellent manners.

There is only one sane social attitude to take in the dealings of Haitian and American. The American must remember, as he should when he travels anywhere, that he is dealing with foreigners. He must value them according to their own standards and live his own life according to the standards of America. Let the American in Haiti, if he does not care to mix with the Haitians, not do so, but when he meets them treat them as their education and culture entitles them to be treated.

The Haitians understand well the attitude of the Americans. They saw the failure of the attempts in the early days to mix freely. They now are anxious to meet the American men but wait for the Americans to take any initiative in a social way.

In Port-au-Prince there is the American Club, whose membership is limited to Americans. It is situated on Tourgeau Street, one of the main residential streets, and has a most attractive clubhouse. Beside it there are two excellent clay tennis courts, where each afternoon the men play and are later joined for bridge or conversation by the ladies. Opportunity there is, too, for rum punches and cocktails, for Haiti is one of the "wet islands."

Every other Saturday night and in between time upon the arrival of a foreign warship or some occasion of this kind, dances are held at the Club at which either the Gendarmerie band or a small native string orchestra play.

The foreign personnel in Haiti consists chiefly of the Marine officers and treaty officials and their families. This is supplemented by members of the diplomatic corps and business men who are either engaged in business in Haiti or who are there looking over the country in view of future investments. And so there is a good-sized foreign colony, mostly American, in Port-au-Prince, which has a social life all of its own.

There are two chief Haitian clubs—the Cercle Bellevue and the Port-au-Prince. The latter is a young men's club and is located on the Champ de Mars next to Brigade Headquarters. The Cercle Bellevue is the more representative and has a beautiful building in the upper part of town. Its members number as well as the Haitians, certain Americans who have been invited to join. Frequent dances are given by the Cercle Bellevue and they are, like all Latin American parties, far gayer and more elaborate than the American ones. Rarely does a party break up before 5 a.m.

Nowhere in the world could more elaborate and yet correct entertainments be given than the Haitians have. During my visit the Argentine warship "Nuevo de Julio" came into

Port-au-Prince and was the occasion for many entertainments, among them a luncheon to the American officers which was held on board and to which I was invited. It was one of the most delightful luncheons to which I have ever been. That night a state dinner was given by the Minister of Foreign Affairs, M. Barau, to the Argentine Officers, and to which the American Commanding Officer and the Officer of the Gendarmerie were also asked. Mme. Barau is French while her husband is of course a Haitian. No dinner anywhere, I was told, could have been given which would have been more appropriate or more delightful.

The national standard coin of Haiti is a gourde, which is worth 20 cents in American money. It is made in the form of our American dollar, and means to the Haitian about what a dollar means to an American. About two years ago there was a scarcity of gourdes.

An attempt was made to have others printed, but as the printing is done in Washington and at that time the printers' strike was in full swing, it was impossible to get the gourdes for a long time. This led to great hoarding of the gourdes, which resulted in their becoming even scarcer and finally in their depreciation to below 4 for a dollar. New gourdes were being given out when I arrived and they were back at their normal value of 5.

The shops in Port-au-Prince are mostly Haitian. The West Indies Trading Company, an American concern, it is true, has two large stores at which much that is in American department stores can be purchased. But the rest are mostly native-owned. Simon Vieux is the leading grocery, and knick-knacks and odds-and-ends of every description can be gotten at "Le Paradis des Dames," "Aux Cents Mille Artiles," and "L'Ange Gardien."

Haiti: Its Dawn of Progress

It was indeed with tremendous regret that I finally left Haiti the first week in February. Haiti, as I have shown, has a wonderful past in the commerce and cultivation of the French days and in the accomplishments of the heroes who made and kept her independent. But these records are only a preface to what a marvellous future she should have. Haiti is essentially a land of the future and of possibilities of which to-day we see only the barest vision. The curtain has already begun to rise upon Haiti as an agricultural land of the first class and more and more it will be opened up and become again the rich country which it once was. And in the future the Haitians and foreigners together will reap the benefit and they will be of great mutual aid to one another.